Affirmations
PUBLISHING HOUSE

living words

First published in 2008
Second printing 2009
Third printing 2010
Copyright © Affirmations Australia Pty Ltd MMVIII

All rights reserved

Published by
Affirmations Australia Pty Ltd
34 Hyde Street, Bellingen NSW 2454 Australia
t: +61 2 6655 2350
e: sales@affirmations.com.au
www.affirmations.com.au

Designed and Edited by
Suzanne and Barbara Maher

10 9 8 7 6 5 4 3

ISBN 978-0-9804060-6-1

Printed in China on recycled paper using Soya based inks.

angels

be
unde

Angels exist
but sometimes,
since they don't
all have wings,
we call them friends.

I am surrounded by angels,
I call them
my best friends.

We stand close
to each other
hand in hand
showing each other
we understand.

May you always
walk in sunshine.
May you never want for more.
May angels rest their wings
right beside your door.

IRISH BLESSING

The great
blessings of angels
are within us
and within our reach.

SENECA

we ar

You have a guardian angel
Who watches over you,
Everywhere you go
And everything you do.

This gentle silent helper
Is there to be your guide,
To shelter and protect you
And for you to walk beside.

*uided
by love*

Your angel will always help you
Whenever things go wrong.
They'll be the wings
beneath your feet
As life's path you walk along.

Feel this calming presence
Be enfolded by its love,
And let your life be guided
By a power from above.

If instead of a gem,
or even a flower,
we should cast the gift
of a loving thought
into the heart
of a friend,
that would be giving
as the angels give.

GEORGE MACDONALD

Kindness in words
creates confidence.
Kindness in thinking
creates profoundness.
Kindness in giving
creates love.

LAO TZU

Give of yourself
as the angels do,
and wonderful things
will come to you.

RAMADAN

Throw out from yourself
a web of love
and catch in it
all that comes.

LEO NIKOLAEVICH TOLSTOY

Angels have
a hidden agenda...love.

Love is the master key
which opens the gates
of happiness.

OLIVER WENDELL HOLMES

he gates
appiness

Angels are pure thoughts,
winged with
truth and love.

MARY BAKER EDDY

Angels are the gatekeepers
to the soul.

LOVE
is a being
who lives as a possibility
in us all.

expand

Today, see if you can
stretch your heart
and expand your love
so that it touches
not only those to whom
you can give it easily,
but also to those
who need it so much.

May each and
every warm thought
bring a wish
for all the best in life.

For love is heaven
and heaven is love.

Keep company
with angels,
and bring a little heaven
to earth.

Guardian Angel
from heaven so bright,
Watching beside me
to lead me aright,

Fold thy wings round me,
and guard me with love,
Softly sing songs to me
of heaven above.

While we are sleeping,
angels have conversations
with our souls.

our soul

To those who can dream
there is no such place
as faraway.

Angels dream beautiful
visions of the world.

create th

All the peace, wisdom
and joy in the universe
are already within us.
All we need do
is open our eyes.

Dream of love.

uture

There is nothing like a dream
to create the future.

VICTOR HUGO

Silently, one by one,
in the infinite
meadows of heaven,
blossomed
the lovely stars,
the forget-me-nots
of the angels.

HENRY WADSWORTH LONGFELLOW

The beauties of the world
are best seen by those
who strive to reach them.

see magi

The appearance of things
change according to
our emotions.
We see magic
and beauty in them,
but the magic and beauty
are really in ourselves.

KAHLIL GIBRAN

nd beauty

An angel can illuminate
our thoughts and minds
by strengthening
the power of vision.

ST THOMAS AQUINAS

The happiest of people
make the most of everything
that comes along the way.

Life is too important
to take seriously.

Angels can fly
because they
take themselves lightly.

Please notice
when you are happy.

Never drive faster than your guardian angel can fly.

take you

Angels may not come when you call them, but they'll always be there when you need them.

elf lightly

Do all the good you can.

Every human being
feels pleasure
in doing good to another.

THOMAS JEFFERSON

Angels know
how to light the way.

There are two ways
to spread the light:
to be the candle
or the mirror
that reflects it.

EDITH WHARTON

nothin

May you always have
a sunbeam to warm you,
a moonbeam to charm you.
A sheltering angel
so nothing can harm you.
Laughter to cheer you.
Faithful friends near you.
And whenever you pray,
Heaven to hear you.

IRISH BLESSING

I f we were like angels,
the world would be
a heavenly place.

Friendship is a knot
tied by angels' hands.

Angels walk softly
and carry big presence.

An angel
is someone
you feel like you've
known forever
even though
you've just met.

The sound of
an angels voice
can unlock
your hidden feelings.

Surrender to the music.

you

Music is the speech of angels.

THOMAS CARLYLE

the heart

An angel can fly
directly into
the heart of the matter.

The guardian
angels of life
sometimes fly so high
as to be beyond our sight,
but they are always
looking down
upon us.

JEAN PAUL RICHTER

We all have
a little voice inside
that guides us.

let love fil
th

May we live in peace
without weeping.
May our joy outline
the lives we touch
without ceasing.
And may our love
fill the world,
angel wings
tenderly beating.

IRISH BLESSING

Do what makes you happy.

be guided

Seek not to understand that you may believe, but believe that you may understand.

ST AUGUSTINE

May you see
the angels hands
at work in your life.

y your
nner voice

Stay open to all.

In the highest vision
of the soul
a waking angel stirs.

JAMES ALLEN

Be an angel to someone else
whenever you can.

embrace

We are all angels
with one wing,
the only way to fly therefore,
is to embrace
one another.

LUCIANO DE CRESCENZO

Every blade of grass
has its angel
that bends over it
and whispers,
"grow, grow".

*grow,
grow*

Angels encourage everyone
in the right direction…
UP.

Knock on the sky
and listen to the sound.

ZEN SAYING

When hearts listen,
angels sing.

The warmth
of an angels light
can comfort and illuminate
the whole world.

*vith
your heart*

Angels occupy
the loveliest corners
of our thoughts.

Mix a little foolishness
with your serious plans,
it's lovely to be silly
at the right moment.

leave room

Angels paint with sound
and sing with colour.

Always
leave room in your life
for the angels.

Your angel
flies ahead of you,
to guard you along the way.

All angels
come to us disguised.

JAMES RUSSELL LOWELL

Make yourself
familiar with the angels
and behold them
frequently in spirit;
for without being seen,
they are present
with you.

ST FRANCIS DE SALES

may the

May angels rest beside your door
may you hear their voices sing
May you feel their loving care for you
may you hear their peace bells ring
May angels always care for you
and not let you trip and fall
may they bear you up on angels wings
may they keep you standing tall

with

May they fill you with their presence,
may they show you love untold,
may they always stand beside you
and make you ever bold.
May they teach what you need to know
about life here and here-after.
May they fill you always with their love
and give you the gift of laughter.

Titles in this series:

angels
ISBN 978-0-9804060-6-1
happiness
ISBN 978-0-9805377-8-9
friendship
ISBN 978-0-9804060-8-5
dream
ISBN 978-0-9805377-7-2
inspiration
ISBN 978-0-9805377-0-3
well-being
ISBN 978-0-9805377-9-6

Whilst every effort has been made
to acknowledge the author of the quotations used,
please contact the publisher if this has not occurred.

LIGH
en
divine
MESSE
heave
TREASURE